The Art of
Local Advertising

Proven Strategies for Keeping
Customers Loyal in Today's
Competitive Marketplace

By

Connie S. Gorrell

Legal Disclaimers

The Art of Local Advertising

Proven Strategies for Keeping Customers Loyal in Today's Competitive Marketplace

TABLE OF CONTENTS

Introduction

Do you possess the single most profitable art needed in order to run a successful business? It's not keeping the shelves stocked. It's not managing employees. It's not even having a good product.

No. The most important skill is marketing your business. And, make no mistake...it is truly an Art. Why? Because the only time you can bring money into your business is if you actually sell something, be it tangible items or services. You can't stock the shelves or hang your shingle unless you have money to buy the supplies to put on the shelves and keep your business operational.

You can't pay your employees unless you have money coming in from selling your unique services. A great product could as well be a piece of junk in a box if nobody knows it exists.

And that is where effective and targeted marketing comes in. It's the way you artfully communicate to the public that you have a unique product, that you offer a good consumer experience and that they should repeatedly buy from you rather than from your competitors.

Marketing is also the most misunderstood skill on the planet. That's why it is an art—something to be honed, tested and perfected. Poor marketing is why 65% of new businesses close their doors after 2 years, and over 85% of businesses don't make it 8 years before going belly up.

Most of your competition does not understand how to do their own marketing properly in order to bring in amazing results in little to no time. So by knowing a few simple secrets you will be at a great advantage. Isn't that what it's all about?

Remember: In the land of the blind, the person with one good eye is King. Loyalty equates to royalty when it comes to your customers. The trick is letting <u>them</u> know that.

You are about to learn some straightforward, proven, powerful—and profitable—marketing strategies that you can start using today to become the "royalty" in your own local marketplace within 3 months.

You have, right now in your hands, information that could change your life (and your business) forever. Use it wisely and profit from it with my blessings. Let's get started...

With all my best,

Connie Gorrell

Are You Leaving Money on the Table?

Do you know the "Big Three" when it comes to deadly mistakes that almost all small businesses make at some point, if not continuously? If you don't, you are certainly not alone. Most entrepreneurs and business managers simply have never considered the fact that by making three small tweaks to their current business plan, they can increase sales by up to 20% within the next 100 days. It's absolutely true.

I know that some of these ideas will shock you. In fact, I hope they do. Why? Because my job is to help you take a fresh look at your own business, and evaluate the areas that can be improved *right now* in order to create more sales geared to improve your bottom line immediately. It's time you learned the art of successful advertising in today's super competitive marketplace.

This highly competitive climate presents new challenges and—better yet—exciting opportunities for extreme success. Make haste to take full advantage of them.

As you know, customers have more choices than ever, so making savvy marketing and advertising choices can be the difference between consumer excitement about your business, or indifference altogether.

11

First off the bat, it is important to know the differences between Advertising, Marketing and Public Relations. In a nutshell it goes like this:

- **Advertising** is actually paying for ad space in a newspaper, magazine or media outlet such as television, Internet or radio.

- **Marketing** is the promotion of your business through a variety of campaigns such as text messaging, attending trade shows, or sending newsletters or postcards among other things.

- **Public Relations** targets getting your business, services, event or product mentioned in the media

We are going to pull out all the stops as we go sailing on the way over your competition's head. Take that which is pertinent to your business and use the techniques within. The goal is to customize them to your individual business needs.

Before we dive into the nitty gritty of local marketing, allow these few words of advice. There are some great ways to stand out in your local area—head and shoulders above the rest.

Get involved with your community to get more "face time" with your buying public. Collect food or articles of clothing for your local food bank and charities. Sponsor sports teams, a local trash clean-up day or look into planting attractive trees and flowers in public places (check with local officials first). These are also effective ways of getting noticed in the local media. Not bad, for free advertising.

What we discuss in this book may be new methods to you, but read with an open mind. Challenging times call for new ideas! You're creating your masterpiece, after all. Marketing your business in a new way can be quite enjoyable and publically enlightening.

Hint: Smile your way through this process; it will make your competition wonder what you're up to. But seriously, we are going to discuss and discover highly targeted, extremely individualized and unique ways of situating your business to stand out among the rest. One merchant I know wrapped a huge ribbon around the store during their anniversary sale; another put a pig in the window. You could put a bull in your china shop, but it isn't recommended or even necessary. I am going to give you the goods needed to make your company stand out and away from the competition.

The top three mistakes referred to earlier are easily overlooked and misunderstood which is exactly why it is imperative that we discuss them. Here are the three most commonly made mistakes in marketing:

1. Going After New Customers

2. Not Effectively Using Cross-Sells, Up-Sells or Packaged Deal Selling Techniques

3. Not Completely Understanding the Lifetime Value of a Loyal Customer

MISTAKE #1:

GOING AFTER NEW CUSTOMERS

Yes, you read that right. New customers are the *most expensive* people in the world to find, attract into your place of business, and then convert into regular paying customers.

Side Bar: It is wise to consider your current customer base as your best resource for drumming up new business. Word of mouth advertising (whether good or not so good) is very effective within the local community. Set aside a specific amount of time per week dedicated solely to identifying ways to keep your best clients happy with your services. Special Customer Loyalty and Appreciation Programs get great mileage in the race to beating your competition. Your clients tell their friends and family about your business, and when their review is positive the new customers find their way to your doorstep.

To help drive home the importance of your existing customer base, let me demonstrate a powerful fact.

There are only three ways to increase your profit margins. The first way, obviously enough, is to increase your number of customers.

Let's say young Brent has a lemonade stand. He sells 100 cups a day to 100 people and makes $0.10 a cup for a total of $10 a day in profit. If little Brent figures out a way to get 200 people to buy a cup of his lemonade he's just doubled his profits.

But that's not the only way Brent can double his profit. What if he figures out a way for his customers to purchase two cups of lemonade each? By doing this, he will double his profits with the same number of customers.

And what if he were to offer something for his customers to purchase that is complementary to the lemonade, such as a hot dog? Then, if a certain percentage *also* buys a hot dog when he sells them lemonade, Brent significantly increases his sales.

In review: There are three specific ways that you will grow your business and increase profits:

- Add more customers

- Get regular customers who purchase more items each visit

- Get the regular customers to purchase more items each visit *and* offer incentives to entice them to visit more frequently

Of the three, which is the most profitable? Think about it this way: Say you spend $2,500 a year on a Yellow Page ad and it brings you 100 prospective customers.

You have paid $25 for each person that has entered your store who *might* purchase from you. That is a static cost. You pay that $25 if they buy nothing from you, or if they buy everything in the store. Plus, you paid for those consumers that never laid eyes on the ad but happened along anyway.

So what if you could increase the average transaction value of each customer by just $10? What would it cost you? Usually nothing but a few minutes of creative thought. You already paid $25 to get them in the store so you might as well maximize their value.

As in Brent's case, he used what is referred to as "cross-selling" on his patrons for a hot dog. It's just a matter of creatively packing complementary goods and using the right language to get the highest number of people to say yes to purchasing something in addition to what they originally came in to the store to purchase in the first place.

Years ago McDonald's started something big by simply asking one question: "Do you want fries with that?" Extra cost for McDonald's to do that: 2 seconds of training for the employee; 2 seconds for the employee to say it to each customer; 2 seconds for the customer to say yes.

The result: an overall bump of about $0.08 in profit *per customer*. And with "over 1 billion served" that's a pot stocked full of profit!

There are two golden secret rules of thumb to follow and they both deal with your existing valued customer base. Ready?

Golden Rule number 1: *Spend more of your advertising budget, time and energy on finding ways to get customers who have already purchased from you in the past, or your new prospects, to purchase* <u>more</u> *from your business.*

Sometimes the last thing you need is more unattached customers. Whatever problems you currently have in your business usually multiplies when you bring new customers into the funnel. Instead, figure out how to get *more* from the *same* number of your good customers. Besides, the word of mouth advertising that your regular customers do on your behalf is more than enough to bring in the perfect clientele for your business.

Golden Rule Number 2: *You must create campaigns, incentives and specials to entice your existing customers to make more frequent purchases from you.*

Here are customer criteria required in order to make your marketing work optimally well for you:

- Customers have to know you exist

- Customers have to want (and be able to afford) what you are selling

- Customers have to know, like and trust you

Obviously, new customers first need to hear about you. They need to know that your business exists and that your customer experience is second to none. But that's not enough. They also have to be in the market for what you offer. Don't attempt to sell ice cream to Eskimos. Keep your finger on the pulse of your industry by watching for fads and buying trends of your demographic.

And finally, customers have to trust you enough to willingly exchange their hard-earned dollars for the value you promise to deliver to them.

Your current valued customers, on the other hand, already know you exist, and have already demonstrated that they need at least some of what you offer. And at one point in their life they trusted you enough to exchange their dollars for the value you promised them.

All else being equal, who do you think will be more inclined to say yes to your next offer? A stranger? Or someone who knows you and is likely to be comfortable dealing with you again—someone to whom you previously provided a good service experience?

I think the answer is obvious. Before we go into how to get former customers to increase the frequency of which they purchase from you, let's first deal with increasing the average purchasing size from each customer individually.

MISTAKE #2:

NOT EFFECTIVELY USING CROSS-SELLS, UP-SELLS OR "PACKAGE DEAL" SELLING

We have already discussed "cross sells" with the McDonald's "Do you want fries with that?" example. So what could this mean for your business? The first thing you need to do is to design and implement your own cross-sells.

There is a fairly simple way to do that. Look at the five to seven most popular selling items in your business. Each one of them should have a cross-sell. For example in the flooring business (apply the following *concepts* into your particular business type here), when people buy carpeting, you could also have a special offer for them to buy a spot removal product along with their new carpeting.

You can even offer a special "purchase discount" because you don't need as high of margins since you have already paid (in marketing and advertising) to attract them to come in the door and purchase from you in the first place.

Select your five biggest sellers and find other items that you can offer that complement these main purchases just as fries ideally complement a cheeseburger.

Then, simply create a quick script to use and train your employees to use this technique. It could be something as simple as "Would you be interested in receiving a special 60% VIP discount on spot remover to complement your flooring purchase today?"

Anything is better than nothing. Based on tests, even a weak attempt at a cross-sell works 6%-20% of the time. The point is that cross-sells inolve almost no hard cost or effort at all to implement, so why not do it?

The second thing is the *up-sell*. This is where you offer your customer a more premium version of what they are ready to purchase. Let's return to the flooring example.

There are different pads you can put under your carpet. There is the basic pad, often made of several different materials that are bonded together, thus making it cheaper to sell to the client. Then there is "premiere" pad, which is solid, more durable, makes the flooring last longer, but is more expensive.

In this case, when putting together an offer for the customer, you could say something like "Would you like to invest a little bit more to make this carpet last 6 years longer—and feel more comfortable under your feet?"

Then, you simply explain why buying the upgraded version of the padding is a better option for them.

Think about it this way—if your mark-up is the same for both types of padding, you make more money by selling them the more expensive carpet pad. Example: Let's say you make 50% profit on each pad you sell. If a customer needs 100 square yards of the basic pad and that sells for $4.50 per square yard, then you just sold $450 of materials, of which $225 is profit to you.

So bump them up to the premium pad that sells for $7.50 per square yard. That's $750 in material sold, of which $375 is profit in your pocket.

You achieved an increase of $150 for just a few minutes of sales work. Again, all you have to do is come up with a simple script, and a simple way to demonstrate why the little bit of extra cost involved for the customer is worth the investment in terms of what they are going to get for that little extra bit of cost.

So how can you make this work for you? Go back to those five or seven popular products and simply ask yourself, "Is there an upgraded and/or premium version of this that I can offer to my customers?"

The answer is yes: There always is. And often times, you can *create* a premium version without hardly any additional hard cost, if you focus on intangibles. Let me give you an example.

Let's say you own a high-end restaurant. One premium version you can offer to your clients is the "immediate seating" VIP club. For a small fee each year, you can guarantee that these customers get seated as soon as they enter the restaurant.

In this case, you're selling time and convenience, not a product. That has a lot of value in this day and age. People like upgrades and conveniences.

Or you could even create a special area for preferred customers; one that has a much more luxurious climate to it, to allow them to enjoy the atmosphere more. Again, you're selling luxury, not a product... another intangible.

The final sales technique you should consider using is *packaged selling*. Most people prefer to have someone else make the decision for them, so they don't have any responsibility in the matter.

As in the the flooring example, why not create an "Active Lifestyle Package"? This would be for people with young children, maybe pets as well, or for those who have high traffic homes.

For this special package, you choose the carpet, padding, vinyl and tile options, and then sell it as a package, instead of each component on its own. This allows you to already *include* the premium versions, or the products that have the highest profit margins.

Your customers are more likely to say yes, if you do it right, since it's easier for them to say yes when the decisions are made for them.

The next logical step is to up-sell them to an even more deluxe package. In this case it could be the "Active & Luxurious Lifestyle Package."

Going back to our restaurant example, let's design the "Romance Package". In this case, the customer would get a limo to pick them up at their door, they get a special table near the fireplace that is more secluded, they get a vase filled with beautiful flowers to take home as a keepsake, and they get a special "Lover's Dessert" for the lucky couple to share.

You are no longer in the restaurant business. Now you are in the romance business—and you can charge a lot more for that!

At the very least, create one package deal that you can offer to a certain portion of your clients. Make it higher priced and more luxurious than normal so that even if only a handful of customers say yes to it each year, you'll have made a pretty good extra bit of profits without doing hardly any more work. Your marketing consultant can be of value to assist you on this as well.

MISTAKE #3:

NOT UNDERSTANDING THE LIFETIME VALUE OF A LOYAL CUSTOMER

If you knew the potential lifetime value of even one average customer, you would spend far more time making sure existing customers continued to use your services, and far less time trying to get new customers.

Let me give you an example. Let's say Gina is a 40 year old local woman and spends $100 a week at her preferred grocery store. Gina doesn't plan on moving any time soon, and has at least thirty more years of good shopping left in her.

So doing the math, 30 years is 1,560 weeks. And at a *minimal* average of $100 a week in groceries at today's prices, that's $156,000. If you owned that grocery store, don't you think it would be prudent to come up with a strategy to make sure Gina keeps coming back to you? What about Gina's kids who marry and live near-by? They are more lifetime customers, potentially. You stand to gain another generation of loyal customers.

A study done 20 years ago was recently retested and re-confirmed in its accuaracy. Once again, it discovered the causes that resulted with customers not further patronizing a store or a service provider.

Here is what they learned about customer traffic:

- *9% leave to go to the competition*

OK, sure...someone else might come along offering them a better deal, or better service. Or perhaps they have a location that's closer than yours. Though unfortunate, that is part of the game. Nonetheless the instructive thing to recognize is that you only lose 9% of your customers because of this (though there are methods of reducing this as we have discussed and will continue as we go along).

- *9% leave because they move away*

It is hard to get someone to come back to your store if they move halfway across the country. It's just the nature of the beast and today's mobile society. Some will move because we are, by nature, nomadic creatures, especially now.

- *14% leave because of a complaint or dissatisfaction with service or product you provide*

Okay, this aspect can be worked on a bit, but one thing I have learned in business is you can't please everyone, nor do you want to. Anyway, it's not that big of a deal, because there is something far, *far* greater that causes your customers to go somewhere else for services that you provide.

It is greater than all these other factors combined. It pains me to tell you...

68% take their business elsewhere because of perceived apathy of the service provider.

That is something totally avoidable! This is why the issue is so crucial and lead to the sole purpose for the creation of this book.

In other words, they feel you only look at them as someone to get money from, and that you don't really care about them after the sale. Notice the word *perceived*. You know the old saying, "What one perceives to be true *is* their truth."

You might very well care a great deal about them, but if you don't show them you care in a way that's unique and that isn't something that everyone else already does, then there is no reason for them to remain loyal to you. I can speak personally and tell you that I have taken my business elsewhere on several occasions for this very reason. Haven't you?

Sometimes we are simply too busy or feel too overwhelmed to goosh the goodness and ooze excitement over our clients coming through the door. I get that. But knowledge is power and just being aware of how you could be coming across may help you remember to brighten your smile when you address your customers. Make their day brighter, too.

If you don't have a specific customer retention strategy in place, you could be losing two-thirds of your previous customers. When you consider the potential lifetime value of a single customer, that should make you cringe!

So what's the remedy? First, you need to increase the amount of communication you have with your past customers. Design a program that focuses on staying in touch with your customers. Depending on the business you are in, you could consider methods for personal follow up, either by email, phone, hand written letter or in person.

You should also consider a newsletter, and no, not one of those fancy, corporate looking newsletters I'm sure you are familiar with. Take a more personal approach. Let your business' personality shine through.

People don't fall in love with corporations. They fall in love with personalities. The first part of that word is "person". Open up to them. Let them know who you are and a little bit about what's going on in your business. You should show some character and a bit of humor, and style as well as good information and great deals.

Think of why you are close friends with the friends you have chosen in your life. Try to establish that same type of bond with your customers. There are several strategies I use for this purpose, such as creating a monthly newsletter. There are some good copywriters looking for work that can provide you with affordable content if you don't have the time or talent to do it yourself. Talk to your customers, too. You might be surprised of their expertise and willingness to contribute articles for your newsletter.

Finally, someone who cares about you looks out for your best interest with no ulterior motive in mind. Again, that's where a newsletter could come in handy. Each month, you can create an article giving your customers tips on how to better their life, improve the value they can get from your services, and other things that can make them feel better about themselves and their situation. Offer them a special promotion or a discount. They will know they're getting all this just because they are a customer of *yours*!

That's how you make someone feel special.

Do you see why those three issues are considered to be really big mistakes? Realize that they are only mistakes if you fail to heed them. But you are not going to do that. Right?

With all that said, create some type of customer retention campaign. That's often just staying in contact with past customers, even if only once every few months, to let them know you're still thinking about them.

New on the horizon is mobile texting campaigns which are another great way to spread the word on a special offer created especially for your best customers. It's time to get creative!

Here are some other simple suggestions for making your customers feel appreciated (therefore increasing your customer satisfaction and retention levels):

- Offer a 'gift with purchase' program, whether it is a tangible item or a discount

- Coupons are an affordable, effective and easy way to distribute your specials. (Note: If you choose coupons via various means of distribution, remember to code them in such a manner that you can track them upon their return to you. Gage your response rates and you will learn the best media avenues to use).

- "FREE" is an attention-getting, powerful word for sure! Consumers love free stuff! Who doesn't appreciate a small token of thanks; even something as insignificant as a new ink pen is acceptable, but be creative.

- Offer free samples to return customers

Revisit the Big Three Mistakes
...Because They Are Crucial to Your Success

1. **Solely Marketing to New Customers**

2. **Not Effectively Using Cross-Sells, Up-Sells or Packaged Deal Selling Techniques**

3. **Underestimating the Lifetime Value of a Loyal Customer**

Center of Influence Marketing

I will go out on a limb and say that 'traditional' advertising can be a significant waste of money if you are not careful. Why? Because traditional advertising will land you traditional results. You don't become an industry leader or a dominant presence in your community by doing things the traditional way.

Many small businesses are still advertising in the Yellow Pages. But it is becoming quite clear that phone book advertising is weakening significantly, perhaps even becoming obsolete. More people than ever are now using the Internet for their information sources. For instance, one can use today's 'smart phone' (iPhone, Android, etc.) to instantly look up any person or business at the touch of a button. It is crucial that businesses find their footing in the mainstream of today's new mobile marketing capabilities, or unfortunately risk getting left behind by their competition.

Almost all phone book (or any print) ads look the same these days. Take a look. Could it be because they are all designed by the same person or company? Of course, this means that everybody's ad is (by definition) 'traditional' —meaning nondescript. Know that you do not have to simply get in line here and follow blindly.

Newspaper advertising is also lagging behind. But again, almost all the ads look the same. They are designed by the same groups of people. If everything looks the same, everyone gets the same type of results.

Finally, consider this—when advertising in newspapers or phone books, you are advertising in the *same places as your competitors*. Not to sound disrespectful, but...that's kind of dumb, isn't it? I would rather advertise in a vacuum where at least I'd be the only choice. The point is to locate your customers and stand out and away from the crowd so they can easily find you.

Today's marketplace is extremely competitive. You really have to break through barriers, fight your way out of the box, and start thinking while you are out there. I fashion myself as a collector of good ideas. I look for those unique ways of advertising that does not garner just ordinary results, but rather extraordinary results instead.

What I am about to show you is going to give you a far greater return than traditional advertising ever will. It will also dramatically enhance the relationship you have with your fellow business owners. It could make others think that you are some sort of genius because of your innovation in marketing and respected community relations.

I am talking about *Center of Influence Marketing*, and how it can take on many faces.

Here's the premise: Instead of hunting down your ideal prospects, what would happen if you connected with non-competing merchants (where your customers are known to frequent) and worked out a mutually beneficial relation with them? This can be done physically—and virtually.

Physical Locations:

Go where your customers already are instead of randomly (and hopefully) picking them up one by one in the newspaper, on the television or radio, or in the phone book.

So here's what you can do: Identify several different businesses where your ideal customers frequent in large numbers. Then construct an offer that will allow you to siphon those ideal customers off into your own sales funnel.

Let's take a second to talk about *targeted marketing* strategies. Say you and I each owned a pizza parlor. You would only need one competitive advantage, and you could destroy me and win every single customer if you played your cards right.

Targeted marketing isolates and focuses your efforts on singling out those who are "hungriest" for whatever it is that *you* offer.

Let me make it real for you. Let's say you're in the retail flooring business. Okay, now people who buy flooring—what else do they tend to need that complements that?

Many people who need flooring also need paint. What would happen if you had a majority of the paint stores sending the customers who needed flooring your way?

If I wanted to market to small businesses to offer my marketing consultation services, where would I go? Well, it could be that I would start with the local accountants, because they help a lot of business owners with their taxes.

I could also approach the heads of trade associations that small business owners would be a member of (like the Chamber of Commerce, for example), and volunteer to give a free speech where I would share my expertise on how to get more customers. (Note: Do not let the whole speech idea make your knees buckle. You *know* your business; you *know* what you're talking about. Use your expertise to an advantage and take the opportunity to help your potential customers. And imagine everyone in the audience wearing a diaper.)

Our local Chamber of Commerce is very in tune with the needs of local business (especially small businesses) and offers a wide variety of educational and interactive community classes. I highly recommend getting involved with them and other professional or trade groups of peers. Not only is the education worth every penny, the networking opportunities can surprise you.

I would also go to attorneys that help people form corporations and who specialize in helping small businesses. Again, volunteer to speak at seminars. Host a roundtable discussion or an open house for getting folks together. These are proven strategies that work well for gaining respect, visibility and establishing expertise.

Do you see what I'm doing here? I am finding a complementary, non-competitive business entity that already attracts the "hungry" customers that I am in search of. Instead of having to find those customers myself, I'm leveraging on the efforts of others.

It needs to make sense for them to refer others to you before they will actually do so. What is an easy way to do this? Why not say, "Hey, I know from time to time you have customers that also need my services. Let's partner up...combine resources."

In other words, send customers to *them* in return. It could be as simple as creating a promotional flyer to put in their business, and they do likewise to distribute at your business. Now it's a "referral revolving door" and more importantly, it's a win-win situation.

Begin by thinking of five complementary types of industries. Pick the top three businesses in each of them. Now you could have a list of 15 businesses to approach.

Secondly, create your irresistible offer for these businesses. You could come up with something quite enticing that answers their number one question: "What's in it for me?"

Consider creating a special offer just for *their* customers exclusively. It could be a discount, or something extra they get for free for which would normally be charged. This way, the "What's in it for me?" question is answered by the fact that their customers receive special treatment and will appreciate them more. It looks like the owner went to bat and negotiated a special deal just for them.

How many businesses could you do this with? As many as you would like! This can help you acquire new customers, especially when you combine this with referral marketing.

35

You could easily get ten businesses that were complementary to you to promote for you for some sort of incentive, and be respected in the business community for reciprocating.

For some, it might just be that you put up some flyers at the counter, with a special "freebie" coupon just for their customers, and that's okay. For other businesses, it might be a customer exchange. You send customers their way if they send customers to you.

In any case, realize the importance behind this—most of the cost for customer acquisition will only be paid after the customer is acquired. You get referrals because you refer. You can't beat that.

This truly takes the risk out of advertising, because you'll only pay for it when it works. Not a bad deal!

Virtual Locations:

The dawn of the Mobile Marketing era has arrived.

Within this realm of express communication, mass text messaging and optimized mobile websites have become the hottest and most significant of marketing opportunities simply because of the pesky little trend called the cell phone and, to a larger degree, the "smart" phone.

Currently, well over 250 million Americans carry cell phones, and the vast majority of them keep their phones within personal reach at all times—day and night. Your customers' time spent on mobile devises is rising faster than time spent on any other form of multimedia, and that includes the Internet. The statistics are overwhelming, and to *not take full advantage* of these vast and amazng opportunities...? I can't comprehend.

There are over 5 billion cell phone users in the world. But more locally, 2.5 billion text messages are sent each day in the United States alone. To correspond to that, several recent surveys have reported that 98% of text messages are read almost immediately once delivered. The vast majority (91%) of cell phone owners surveyed stated that they keep their phones within reach at all times.

There is payday associated with riding this wave of advertising opportunities. It is here that your customers have taken up residence in their virtual locations.

Mobile Marketing:
Get It While It's Hot!

Mobile Marketing is the latest technology buzz that helps attract more customers—customers that spend more money, and do it more frequently. Mobile Marketing has a proven track record and has shown that people using a mobile browser are further down the purchasing funnel than website browsers and that 55% of them proceed to actually call or go visit a store.

How does it work? By various means, such as by connecting with your customers through SMS (Text) Message Marketing, Mobile Websites, Two-Dimensional QR Codes, Mobile Search Engine Optimization and Mobile Advertising.

It has been proven that text messaging gets almost twenty (20!) times more response rate than that of opening an email. Many of us do not read every email message every day, and there is no guarantee that we will read any specific email initially when there are literally dozens or more waiting in our cluttered in-boxes. Studies revealed that text messages have an astounding 97% open rate. It is a no-brainer to be *virtually* everywhere your customers are by using mass text messaging.

SMS (TEXT MESSAGE) MARKETING

Text Message Marketing is all about timing. It's about sending the right message at precisely the right time. The key to a successful text advertising strategy is to capture local customers (whom have opted in as your loyal customer) in a focused, timely and consistent manner. Your marketing consultant can assist you in targeting your customer campaigns for a specific call-to-action with perfect timing.

Is your restaurant slow on Monday nights? Send out a coupon via a text blast at 4:30p.m. and enjoy a larger crowd for dinner that evening. Did your retail store recently receive a new shipment of a wildly popular item? Send your "preferred customers" a special discount if they come in to purchase today. With a text advertising VIP Club or Preferred Customer Program, you don't have to *hope* that your customers will come in today... you can *entice* them to!

Here is where it gets really good. The days of mobile marketing are just beginning. We are merely cave people at this point—and we have just discovered fire! Less than 5% of businesses have tapped into this next big trend but make no mistake, they will. They will have to, in order to remain competitive. Now is the perfect time for you to get the jump on your competition.

Text messaging has become the number one use for mobile phones—more than calls, more than emails, web-surfing, and even social media combined (though social media such as Facebook and Twitter certainly claim great advertising stakes for your business, too). Today's savvy business owner has social media on their radar screen.

Most text messages are read within an hour. Think about it this way: Do you text?

How many text messages do you receive...and ignore?

If you are like most people, probably none.

Text messages are almost impossible to ignore because when they arrive on your cell phone, they are the ONLY thing visible on the screen. A text message claims its unique space—exclusively and alone. To boot, the text notification envelope stays on the screen until the recipient accesses the text (this also acts as a nice reminder).

A text message marketing campaign might work like this: Your customers opt-in to your text message campaigns by texting a predetermined 'short code' or 'long code' to a specified number arranged by your marketing professional. For instance, if you run a pizza parlor you could post signs or table tents in your establishment that say, "Text PIZZA to 42474 to join our club and receive coupons and special offers from us!" It is important to note that in order to comply with federal law we must also let the customer know that standard text rates may apply and opt-out instructions are offered should they wish to do so.

Staying with the food service industry example, you could blast out this bulk text campaign:

Show this TEXT to your server & receive a Free Appetizer on Tuesday between 4p.m. and 6p.m. Forward this friends and they can enjoy it, too!

Be aware that about one in five business-texted offers get forwarded to the recipients' friends and colleagues thus increasing your response rate. If you make the offer special enough or enticing enough, trust me, they will come (and bring their friends, too!).

Contrary to past beliefs, it's not just those whacky teen-agers and twenty-somethings driving this trend any more. It's *all* active people. Business people, parents, students, the butcher, the baker and the... well, you get the picture. It is all of us. It's probably you, and for sure heckfire—it's me, too.

In a tough economy, your customers appreciate a good deal at their favorite establishments and your bottom line will appreciate the added business. It is widely known that American families enjoy eating out several times a week, meaning—they are going to eat *somewhere*... why not meet up at *your* place?

Send out that text blast and jog your loyal customer's memory. Remind them that you are there—ready and waiting to serve them well.

MOBILE WEBSITES

In addition to text message marketing there is the ability for websites to become optimized especially for mobile phones that are specifically targeted toward local businesses. Available applications, known as apps, abound by the thousands.

Many small business owners hesitate when it comes to securing a mobile website for their business. Missing the unlimited opportunities afforded you by implementing mobile optimized sites could be perceived as dismissing the needs and convenience of your customers. It is very important to offer a user friendly mobile site that is fast and inexpensive for the customer to load. We are a mobile society and to be clear, local customers are doing very specific mobile searches looking to fill their wants and needs.

Appreciate the fact that the mobile surfer is seldom just 'surfing around.' He has a specific goal when he is searching on his mobile phone—to find what he is looking for whether it be directions on how to get to your store or how to purchase your product or service. The most important aspects, however, are the ability to be found in the first place, the site's content and how it is presented.

The needs and behaviors of a mobile surfer differ greatly from an Internet surfer. Statistics show that mobile surfers are further down the purchase funnel than Internet surfers. This means mobile searchers are poised and more ready to take specific buying action such as calling you or visiting your store after viewing your information on their mobile browser.

When making the decision on whether to invest in an optimized mobile website, consider these five ferocious facts:

1. **Customers are looking for your services** (or those of your competitor when they can't find *you!*) on their mobile devises, whether you have a mobile site or not.

2. The **customer will find your competitors' sites** if your website is difficult to find or costly to navigate. Guaranteed.

3. Your **business could be perceived as being behind the times** if lacking the latest mobile technology.

4. **A misinformed customer is an unhappy one.** By choosing no mobile optimization for your website, understand what you are loosing. When the customer attempts to open your website in their mobile browser he may be greeted with a slow and costly download with incomplete layout making it impossible to find the information he seeks. In frustration, he clicks away and on to see what your competitor's mobile site can do for him. I have done this many, many times.

5. In a world where most everyone owns a mobile phone, ***brand perception and brand loyalty is everything***. This could be a problem for you if your website is not mobile friendly.

QR CODES

You probably spotted jumbled-looking boxes on major print ads. These are 'QR Codes' which are a two-dimensional barcodes that can be scanned and read by a camera on a mobile devise that takes you directly to a website, video, Facebook page, or any message or map. QR means 'Quick Response' and it functions as a hyperlink. QR Codes began in Japan and spread through Europe, but has finally found its way to the USA.

The cloaked message can be accessed simply by pointing your mobile phone (or other camera-enabled mobile devise) at the code. If the device has QR Code decoding software installed it will read the code and lead straight to the desired and prearranged destination. Apps for scanning these codes are available at the phone's app store, free of charge.

Here is one of mine:

This QR Code is directed at one of my own websites
www.conciergemobilemarketing.com.

A restaurant customer can use their cell phone equipped with a QR reader to scan the specialized code while waiting for their order to arrive. They could be taken directly to your business website or Facebook page. When they land on your Facebook page, you can have it set up to highlight a special offer or a coupon for them if they "Like" you and become your Fan.

A QR Code can also be configured to contain a phone number, an SMS (text) message, V-Card data or just plain alphanumeric message. This could get fun! You are only limited your imagination. The creative and marketing possibilities are endless.

In one instance I supplied a client with tee shirts for his wait staff to wear. The only thing pictured on the shirt (besides the restaurant's logo) was a QR Code. When the customer used their cell phone to scan the code they found that it simply said, *"Text GREAT FOOD to 42474 and receive special offers and coupons from us."* QR Codes turn plain print advertising into interactive suspense and can be linked to target rich environments. Advertisers can use multiple barcodes tied to different campaigns or destinations to engage their customers multiple times. What a conversation piece!

Listed below are suggestions on how to use a QR Code to benefit your business marketing campaigns:

Website URL	Text Message	Plain Text
Email Address	Email Message	Google Maps
Facebook	YouTube	Twitter
PayPal	Events	Contact Details
iTunes	Telephone Number	WiFi

MOBILE SEO & MOBILE ADVERTISING

When you have a mobile website you can utilize Search Engine Optimization (SEO) to broaden your brand's exposure. This means using specific keywords to describe your business to make it easier for your customers and potential customers to locate you on the Internet. For our purposes here, the take away message is that sales conversion rates from mobile advertising are usually 2.7% - 5% higher than that of traditional affiliate advertising. Definitely worth consideration.

Another thing to consider are display banners and inserts within text messaging and searches. Any combination of these forms of mobile advertising will invite a consumer to engage in various forms of mobile media: SMS text, mobile Web, apps and click to call. Best of all, the price for mobile advertising is a fraction of the cost of desktop paid advertising campaigns, but I caution you to seek the assistance of a marketing professional unless you are very well versed in these types of marketing measures.

Let's apply what we know so far:

Generally targeted phone book print advertising is dead or dying; newspapers are choking for readers; billboards get ignored; TV and radio ads cost a small fortune (with zero guarantee that your targeted audience is paying attention). Most local business owners are unsure of how to fill the "advertising gap" that leaves them digging deeper for new ideas every day. If you feel like you have dug to China and don't know where to turn, read on—or call me.

By adding mobile marketing and embracing the possibilities of bulk text message marketing in cooperation with optimized mobile websites to your marketing and advertising repertoire, you have found your unique ticket to exclusivity!

How to Find Customers for Life

Imagine that there was a huge amount of oil buried outside in your backyard, right under your nose. We're talking millions of dollars worth.

Would that make you rich? No, not if you didn't know about it! You could live your entire life sitting on "liquid gold" and be none the wiser.

However, if I told you about it and showed you beyond a shadow of doubt that there was indeed oil located there you could drill to find it. You would be filthy rich.

In most businesses there exists a situation similar to the oil well example above. Small business owners are sometimes sitting on a potential fortune but they don't realize it. The tricks of the trade involve getting the customers to mentally think of your business first when it's your special services they seek.

In this chapter I am going to share with you perhaps the single most effective strategy for mining the hidden gold that is likely to exist in your business.

First, know your market inside and out. Know it better than your competition. Learn who your customers are before you spend a dime on directing any advertising to them. Talk to the movers and shakers in your local community; read your trade journals as they are filled with useful information; watch the news for consumer buying trends.

A second proven strategy is to study your competition. Once you have a good picture of who they are and what their business is about (their store layout, pricing structure, advertising strategies, return policies, product services—or lack thereof), you can determine their vulnerabilities and cash in on them for your own business. Don't be shy on this one.

Third, socially network within local business and community groups as well as with your competitors. You might be surprised how loose-lipped they can become by saying too much about their upcoming products, specials or services.

In the past, I have suggested to some of my clients that it could be wise to comprise a focus group consisting of a few of their best customers. The group is asked to discuss what they like or don't like about the business' products or services. Ask targeted questions and you will receive targeted information in return. The group could tell you quite a bit about your company, and even more about your competition in the process.

This method is great for local market research. It makes the chosen few feel much more important and maintains their loyalty to your brand because they have established a sense of ownership at that point. This may not be the scientific approach...but it works.

Take advantage of the competitive edge your customers can offer, simply by seeking out their insight. Having this type of information in your hip pocket can be powerfully effective!

THE "FORGOTTEN RULE" OF AN
OBSCURE ITALIAN ECONOMIST

In 1906 a man by the name of Vilfredo Pareto discovered something unusual about the Italian economy—80% of the wealth was controlled by 20% of the population. The 80 / 20 Rule.

Was this just an anomaly? Turns out it was not. In Britain he found the same thing to be true and went on to find it to be true in pretty much all economies he examined. But what is interesting is that this unequal distribution exists outside of economies as well. For example, studies have shown in general that:

80% of traffic accidents are committed by 20% of drivers

80% of crimes are committed by 20% of the population

80% of a company's output comes from 20% of its employees, and most importantly of all...

80% of your profits come from only 20% of your customers!

This rule almost always rings true. So what does this mean for you—and for your business?

Simply put: If you can isolate who your "20 percenters" are, and then come up with a marketing plan that will attract more customers like those "20 percenters" and also create additional products, services and offers for your "20 percenters" then...

You should be able to, very easily, add 20% to your bottom line profits within the next 90 days.

WHERE TO START

Depending upon your type of business, in an ideal situation, you have probably kept track of your past customers' purchases. You know what your top selling products are. What you want to do now is go through and isolate those customers who have spent the *most* money with you. These are the ones that know, like, and trust your business.

Obviously that doesn't necessarily mean that they are your most profitable customers. They are just your highest grossing customers. Unfortunately, gross does not always mean more profits. However, it is a good place to start.

After you find your highest grossing customers, analyze your profit margin on those customers, to narrow it down even more. To make it easy for you, come up with your fifty highest grossing customers, and out of those fifty, arrange them in order of most profitable.

Now take your twenty *most profitable* customers, and analyze them. What we are looking for are trends of demographics and psychographics.

Demographics are things such as:

- Size of Household

- Annual Income Earned

- Age

- Gender

- Geographical Location

Psychographics are:

- What clubs they belong to

- What their hobbies and interests are

- Their values and opinions

- Their shopping habits

- Lifestyle & other behavior attributes

In other words, you are trying to isolate their "culture" if you will.

53

How can this be helpful to you? Let's say you analyze your results and find out that your most profitable customers are typically:

Aged 45-50, have 2-3 children, are married, live on the northeast side of town, make between $75,000 to $100,000 a year, are active in the community, especially with charitable events, typically play a lot of golf and/or tennis, and take 2-3 vacations a year.

That's some valuable information! For starters, did you know you can rent a list in your area with those "selects" (select is just a fancy term for different attributes).

Yes, for a fee you could get a list of all the people in your city that are between 45-50, living in a certain zip code, making an annual income of $75,000 to $100,000 a year. And that's just a few of the "selects" you can specify. You can even go deeper if you wish.

These are the type of prospects you want to concentrate on with your marketing dollars. While past results do not necessarily guarantee future behavior, they are about as good an indicator to go by as any. The point is, if that type of customer was profitable to you in the past, it stands to reason similar people who fit that description will also be extremely profitable for you now as well.

The best thing to do next is to create a direct mail campaign and send a letter to each name on your list making them a special offer (unless you opted to utilize text advertising whereas saving paper and postage budgets).

You want to write an advertisement that is personable, explains the benefits of your services, and makes a special "introductory offer" to get them back into your place of business. You can also add beneficial advertising information in your newsletter.

In the advertisements address things like golf and tennis, taking vacations, saying things that your identified demographics are known to associate with, and talk about charitable events. This helps build rapport with the prospect. You just have to tie those things to your sales message and special offer in some creative way.

That's just one simple example of how to make the 80/20 Rule work in your favor.

Here's an even better example: Look into your customer records of your most profitable customers and ask yourself, "What services and goods can I offer them that they don't currently have, but would be complementary to purchases they've made in the past?"

If someone is a very profitable customer to you, it usually means that they like doing business with you, need a lot of what you have to offer, trust you, and often think of you as the "go-to" solution for problems related to your area of service and expertise.

So if you have a good recommendation that could help bring them value to their life, and fits perfectly for something you have offered them in the past, you're likely to meet with success.

There are several methods that will assist you in maximizing your efforts. Start with your top twenty customers. Write them each a personal letter. Start with letting them know that you were analyzing your past records and noticed that they have been a very good and valued customer. Then say you also noticed something that may be a benefit to them based on their past purchases. Add that since they have been such good customers, you are going to give them a special deal next time they come into the store and purchase something. Give them specific examples, such as:

"I noticed you purchased (xx) from us. We wanted to let you know that we have a new product that complements (xx) perfectly, so if you come in within the next two weeks I can give you a special deal of 30% off the regular price. This is just our way of saying thank you for being such a valuable customer."

Another strategy to consider is the referral strategy. People typically hang around others who share their same values and beliefs. This is a perfect way to attract new customers who are likely to be just as profitable as those have have identified as your past most profitable customers.

In this case, send your best customers a letter and let them know that you're making them a "valued customer special offer," If they were to recommend someone to your business you will give their referrals a "preferred VIP discount" or "preferred VIP treatment" since they came from a highly valued source.

People love to refer when this is the case. It makes them look good in front of their friends. A lot of people find value in that. It's also great for you, because word of mouth advertising is some of the *best advertising* there is. And if you can just get these referrals into the door and have them start a buying relationship with you, chances are they will continue to buy from you in the future. Thus you will get more than just a one-time purchase; you may get a customer for life with a high lifetime value.

As a case in point on a personal level: After injuring my lower back while blow-drying my hair, (yep...don't ask...) one of my employees referred me to a local business which happened to be owned by her cousin. This facility specialized in massage therapy and various spa services. Being in agony with any attempted movement, I made an appointment and hobbled in. After only two therapy sessions I was amazed at how much better my back felt—I could actually move without squeaking. (My husband said I made "squeaking noises" when I attempted any movement. Sexy, huh?)

After that I began keeping a regular monthly appointment for a therapeutic and relaxing massage because I loved the benefits of massage. The price was right, the services were wonderful and I appreciated being treated like a valued customer. I started referring anyone that would listen to me to this business so that friends and acquaintances could enjoy the same satisfaction in which I reveled—not to mention that I received fifteen minutes *free* on my next massage as a 'thank you for the referral.'

That Christmas, to my surprise, I walked in for my regular appointment, and sitting on the counter was a beautifully presented gift basket filled with spa products—for *me!* The attached card spoke of the owner's appreciation for the referrals I had sent their way over the course of the year.

Needless to say, I know the value of customer loyalty. I am their client for life! That was about six years ago and I still feel special when I walk in. The owner, Kathleen, proved to be very approachable and open to suggestions and listened intently when we asked for a monthly "girlfriend special". To this day, my friend and I go every month (at *least* once) for a spa day. Life's little necessities, you know. It's a rule. We can't break it.

(P.S. My husband also tells me he thinks I make up the rules as I go along).

...But I don't squeak any more.

The Referral Marketing Goldmine

THE POWER OF "WORD OF MOUTH" ADVERTISING

Referrals are the least expensive, yet most effective marketing tactics in the world. We are best advised to respect word of mouth advertising because that door can swing two ways—and one of those ways can hurt a business' reputation in the local community considerably. By delivering the services you promise, you keep your customers happy and they are delighted to share their good experiences with their extended family, friends and colleagues.

The idea is that you should be generating a large portion of your new customers by marketing to existing customers. You simply cannot put a price on the value of your existing loyal customer base. Read that again.

There are several reasons why nurturing a referral program is the smart thing to do. First, quality attracts quality. Psychologists say that you are basically a combination of your five closest friends. In other words, people will refer people who are similar to them.

So if you have a big spender, then guess what? They will most likely refer other big spenders. Every good customer should be actively pursued for a referral because they will

59

usually generate other customers of equal quality and value.

Also, marketing is usually met with skepticism. That is mainly because you are often tooting your own horn in order to get the business. But what if someone else was tooting your horn for you?

Know this—people are more likely to believe in you if someone else endorses your quality than if you brag about your own qualities (awesome as your qualities may be).

What you are really doing is leveraging off of someone else's credibility. People who take the recommendations of their friends are now coming to you with a preconceived notion that you are already quality—before you even have to open your mouth.

Finally, word of mouth marketing is laser target marketing. Basically, you are only going to be getting people who are already in the market for the type of services you are offering. Mass marketing does not have this effect. If you run an ad on television, you are targeting every single person who watches TV. Period.

Adversely, with referral marketing, you're pretty much getting only people who are already a great match to your products or services. This means your closing rate will go up without having to learn one single bit of salesmanship. You are just getting people who are already more likely to say "yes" before they even enter into the store.

Note an important rule of thumb when it comes to referral marketing. Every good customer should get at least three direct chances to refer someone else to you. If you are providing excellent services, this won't be difficult to achieve.

I have found in order to get the best results you have to ask someone three times to make a referral on your behalf. If you do nothing else, you should do this.

To really make it effective, there are two crucial tasks at hand: Make it *easy* for them to refer and make it *worthwhile* for them to refer. This is a double edged sword designed to leverage your efforts much more in-depth than you could believe possible. I am going to show you how to do all of this and more, as I outline what I have found time and time again to be a profit pulling monster when it comes to referral systems.

THE REFERRAL SYSTEM, STEP BY STEP

First, get your metrics in order. How much money can you afford to spend on marketing for the next month? Whatever it is, devote the largest portion of it to your referral marketing.

Step one, identify your budget. Of course much of this depends upon your type of business services and categories.

The specific plan I am going to lay out to you is going to cost around $8 per person to perform. So if you have a budget of $800 for targeted marketing, then you can reach 100 people.

Start small and scale up—that's my best advice. Don't spend too much upfront until you get back some reliable figures, and you can do some testing. Since this is a system, every dollar you spend will be tracked and traced back to determine the return on your investment.

Here's how it works. Someone comes in and purchases an item or service from you. Immediately the next day, you send them a letter in the mail. You thank them, ask for the referral, make it easy for them to refer, and then make it worth their while.

The most important part is that you have enabled it to be in their best interest to refer others to you. For that to happen, first and foremost you must have provided quality and value. So I am going to assume you are performing good service and living up to your end of every deal—this time and every time.

Second, consider that small gifts work wonders (remember the gift basket from my favorite spa?). The best kind of gifts are those that either cost me nothing or very little, but have a huge perception of value. Without a doubt, there is one gift I can consistently create for basically nothing, and it always does the trick.

Coupon Books

This is the Center of Infulence Marketing theory at its finest. It works like this: Approach various business owners and colleagues and tell them that you want to help make sure your mutual customers continue to shop locally. (You could even engage a college student to help make the initials calls for you).

As a thank you gift for your customers, you would like to gift them with coupons or special offers from other local merchants. This equates to providing your customers with added value while keeping their patronage local in cooperation with your fellow business managers.

At that point, simply ask your colleagues if they have any coupons or any special offers that they would like to contribute to your "customer gift book". Cross-marketing with other businesses complementary to yours usually works quite well.

Almost every business owner you talk to will want to take you up on this joint venture. Why? Simple! Because most businesses are not good at doing their own marketing, and to make up for it they always have a special offer, or are willing to do anything if it means getting a few more customers in the store.

You only need to get fifteen or twenty unique coupons offers to make a great gift book. You could accomplish this within a few hours. These are all tactics that your marketing consultant can perform for you as well. After all, you are quite busy running your successful business, anyway.

Now you have a great gift that you can give to anybody who sends a referral your way. How much did this cost you? Merely the cost to print the coupons and mail them or hand distribute them. You just made a gift of high perceived value (everybody loves discounts) that costs you about a dollar to create and a few hours of sweat equity. It is worth the while.

Now let's take a look at what the first referral letter could look like. Of course, feel free to customize this with your own type of flair!

Dear Carol Customer,

We want to say thank you from the bottom of our hearts for doing business with us. If there is anything you need from our services in the future, please do not hesitate to call.

You may not realize this, but the lifeline of our business comes from referrals. If you happen to know anyone else who would benefit from our services, I'd be extremely honored to help them in any way.

If the person you refer becomes our customer, as a token of my appreciation I will send both of you my special valued customer gift book, which has a total of over $250 off coupons for discounts from local business of all kinds!

It's really easy to refer someone to us. I've enclosed two of my business cards with your name written on the back. Please give them to anyone you think could use our services. Just have them present the business card when they come in, so we know it was you that referred them!

Anyway, I just wanted to say thanks again for doing business with us!

Many Thanks,
Lee,Business Owner

There is a lot of psychology that is going on in this first letter that I don't want you to miss.

First, it's personal and it's sincere. How many businesses have you bought something from in the last sixty days from which you received a personal thank you letter in the mail? One or two, you say? None?

Amazing.

Imagine the kind of impact that your letter has when it lands in your customer's mailbox. Huge impact. It says you care. It says you remember them. Do you remember why most people leave a service provider?

Sadly, some pass away. Some may have to relocate. Others leave because of an unresolved complaint or situation. A handful will be stolen away by a competitor. Add all those up, and guess what?

It usually only comes to 32% of all total customers who leave you. So what about the other 68%?

They leave simply because you have never taken the time or initiative to recognize them as something more than a customer.

Pop quiz: It is a busy day in your store or office, but as usual, issues abound. Choosing to deal with only one of the following, which would it be?

  a. An unresolved complaint

  b. A direct competitor in your store trying to steal your customer

  c. The opportunity to let a recent customer know you care about them

You are best served to choose the third option because remember...roughly only 9% leave because of competition, and only 14% leave because of unresolved complaints.

If you do nothing else but keep in contact with your past customers and treat them as your friends and acknowledge them once in a while, you will be putting the "golden lasso" on the remaining 68% of your customers. This will allow you to keep selling to them again and again. That builds customer loyalty. So please—if they give you their loyalty, treat them like royalty.

First, if you get nothing else out of the referral letter, you will get personal communication that will separate you from 90% of all businesses and almost every single one of your competitors.

The second thing the referral letter does is conveys your expectations. You *expect* all of your customers to refer. Most people don't refer simply because they don't know you want them to refer. In fact, I've had customers come up and tell my clients, "Heck, I thought you already had enough customers...I didn't know you could take on more."

Insert quote of Homer Simpson, "Doh!"

You should have seen that business owner slap his forehead. It left a mark.

Once people know that you *want* them to refer, you automatically increase the chances they *will* refer—even if it isn't immediate. Again, I have had people hold on to business cards for two or three years before they gave one to someone else.

Notice the casual tone of our referral letter. People prefer doing business with friends, and not faceless corporations.

Finally, it shows you care. The above letter basically says, "Hey, I know you're busy and I know you got to look out for your own self interests. That's why I have gone the extra mile to make it in your own self interest to refer to me."

Ideally, you don't want to take the above letter word for word. You want to fill in "our services" with your actual services and so forth. But I give you permission to take most of the above verbatim and use it.

But don't stop there. After the first letter one is sent out, wait a couple of weeks. If you haven't gotten a referral from them go for contact number two.

> *Dear Carol Customer,*
>
> *I recently sent you a special letter of thanks and appreciation for your recent purchase. We have delivered several of our special gift books in the last few weeks to valued customers who referred their friends to us. To make sure you don't miss out on your own special gift book, I have enclosed two more business cards with your name on the back, just in case you need them.*
>
> *Give these to a friend in need, and we'll mail your customer gift book right away!*
>
> *Once again, I want to say thank you for being our valued customer, and I hope that we can continue to provide you with more great service in the years to come.*
>
> *Thanks,*
>
> *Lee, Business Owner*

Here is what I know about marketing: One-shot advertising is not very effective. It's not that people don't want to act on your offers. A lot of them do. What happens is that the details of day-to-day living get in the way, and what they intend on doing ends up getting pushed to the back of their mind. We all know how that goes, only all too well.

What this letter does is thank them again, puts you in front of them again, and basically let's them off the hook. It wasn't their fault. You know they're busy people!

Also, it gives you another excuse to send them two more business cards. It also offers some social proof that "everybody else is referring" and makes it more the thing to do.

Every time we track these campaigns, we usually find these types of responses:

- 3% to refer off the first letter

- 4% to refer off the second letter

- 2% to refer off the third.

In any case, all mailings are profitable. If we had stopped after the first letter, we would have gotten a mere 3% response rate. But instead we got 9% total! In most scenarios, it almost always plays out that the second letter will work the best. Who knows why; it just does.

For those customers that do not respond to the first or second letters, consider sending a brief third note:

Dear Carol Customer,

Hope everything is going great for you! I have a few customer gift books left over and I didn't want them to go to waste, so I have enclosed your gift book. It is just our way of saying thank you for being a great customer. I've also enclosed two more business cards with your name on the back.

Just pass them on to a friend if they're ever in need of any of the services that we offer. We'll make sure to treat them right.

With Our Sincere Thanks!

Lee, Business Owner

I don't want you to confuse the technique with the strategy. This truly works because:

- It puts you in front of them 3 times

- It conveys the expectation that they will refer a friend

- It is personal, relaxed and friendly

- It is very easy to do

- It is in their best interest to put it to use; who doesn't appreciate a good deal?

You don't have to do the coupon gift book. Sometimes I'll just purchase tickets for a special upcoming local event, golf, movie, or event complimentary dinners at a good restaurant— anything your demographic may enjoy.

Lastly, a few more pointers:

Make your letters look like personal letters. This means when you design the layout, don't put a fancy "brochure" feel into it. Just picture how you would design the letter if you were going to sit down and write someone a personal note.

When you get this system in place, you'll get some numbers. You might find for every 5 customers you do this for, you get 1 referral in the next 30 days. Okay, do that math—let's say your average sale netted you $100 in profit.

And let's say when you deduct all marketing expenses for creating and mailing the letters, it cost you $100. That's a 5 to 1 return on investment! Try getting that with other types of advertising.

This type of marketing also allows you to perform what is referred to as split-tests. What would happen if you altered the gift? You can literally test every element you want to learn what is working and what is not working. This means you can figure out the exact combination of steps for getting the greatest return on your advertising investment.

Tearing Down
Customer Resistance

How many of the people who walk into your business, or who take an interest in your products and services, end up making a purchase? As you know, in sales this is called a closing rate.

To manage any activity, you first have to measure it. That way you know where you stand in terms of productivity, so you know what you need to do to improve it.

Here is a simple question you need to answer: If 10 prospects are interested in doing business with you, on average how many out of those 10 end up doing business with you?

The percentage itself is not important. In stores with a lot of traffic, you can do 1 out of 10 and be fine. I have a client with website where they do 1 out of 100, and it is good enough for them to make a good return on their investment, because it takes hardly any time or effort. In some businesses, you need 5 out of 10 just to have a chance at making a profit.

While the actual percentage may not be that important, it is important is to know how to improve your percentages to a more acceptable or desirable range. If you get 5 out of 10, do the math and see how much more you would make if you got 6 out of 10. Since they are already coming through your door, most of the work is done. You're just looking for those "little things" to get more people converted into customers.

There are a lot of different ways to improve your closing rate and some are more complicated than others. I always look for the "80/20" factor in any given task. In other words I'm looking for that one or two key things that will make most of the difference between someone purchasing...and not. Here is some insight to help you discover that "one vital fact" that gives you a majority of your results.

Do you know what three criteria are required before a prospect becomes a customer? Knowing this will give you the answer you need. Here are the three all important components:

1. They have to want what you offer.

2. They must have money to purchase it.

3. They need to believe that you'll come through on your end of the deal.

The more inclined they are to already want what you have the easier it is to sell to them. The more money they have set aside for making consumer purchases, the easier it is to the sell to them. The more they believe that you actually will deliver on your offer, the easier it is to sell to them.

I have before me a phone book with Yellow Page ads. I'm going to flip through it and quote some phrases. Here are just a few (and a sample of skeptical consumer thoughts that may accompany the ads):

- **"Dependable & Quality Service"**

  Your typical savvy potential customer is thinking:

  "Oh, yeah!? Prove it, pal."

- **"Value, Service & Convenience"**

  This description is meaningless, and everybody knows it. We may think:

  "Convenience for whom? ...You or me?"

- **"Friendly Service"**

  Once again, consumers have heard this all before, and think:

  "Yeah, right! I've heard that song before."

- **"In Business Over 100 Years"**

  "Longevity doesn't guarantee current technology"

In other words, these are hollow phrases of puffery that everybody uses. It is so easy to say those things, and saying them has become to mean so very little. I've actually called a business whose Yellow Page ad said "friendly service" only to be treated rudely by the receptionist who answered the phone. Guess someone forgot to give her the memo. And whether you think it fair or not, that is a direct reflection on your business as a whole. That is another book to write, but hire carefully!

So how do you go beyond mere puffery and actually prove your case that you are friendlier, more valuable, offer better service and are more dependable than every other option they have available?

Allow me to share with you one simple way to do this that will drastically differentiate you from every competitor, both directly and indirectly. As a bonus, it is very simple to do; it is extremely cost effective and when compiled, can be used in a variety of different outlets and mediums. What I am referring to is customer testimonials.

THE SELLING POWER OF TESTIMONIALS

If you want to increase your closing rates without resorting to any fancy tricks or learning a bunch of new skills, just start being an avid collector of testimonials.

I don't care what anyone else says, they work.

Consider this—what if I told you I was the greatest marketing consultant of all time? Would you really believe me? What if your friend called you up and told you I was the greatest marketing consultant of all time? Then you *might* believe it.

But what if your lawyer, your doctor, your mother, your children's principal, the head of your trade association and the guy you buy bell peppers from at the local farmer's market told you I was the greatest marketing consultant of all time?

I bet you'd be *really* interested in sitting down and having a talk with me, wouldn't you? You'd probably think a great deal more of me than me than from me just calling you up and bragging about my skills.

This is such a simple principle that it makes me wonder why *all* businesses don't use testimonials. I really don't know why. I think it should be a requirement of doing business, personally. That is because, when it comes to raising your closing rates, it makes all the difference.

Now let me show you when, where and how to get these top notch testimonials that will increase the believability of your offers and services.

HOW TO BECOME AN AVID TESTIMONIAL COLLECTOR

If you go searching for opportunities to get testimonials, you will find it is relatively easy and in no time you will begin to collect them.

The best opportunity is when your customer is "in heat", meaning striking while the iron is hot. Let's say you have just done something that has "wowed" them. They might come in to pay their bill and say "I can't believe what a wonderful service you did. It's better than the last five people I've gone to!"

This is your chance! You say: "Thanks! Would it be okay if I shared your story with others who might be interested in our services as well? It really helps us better serve our clients!"

Or, you can say: "Thanks. Would it be okay if I wrote down what you just said and shared it with others? It would mean a lot to me!" Then just write down really quickly what was said, and have them approve it by signing it.

Or you can simply say: "Thanks. Did you know that one of the best ways we get good clients like you is sharing the success stories of our past clients? Would it be okay if we quoted you in some of our marketing and sales communications?"

Do not make this harder than it has to be. The main process is to get them when they are in a good mood. Ask if you can have their permission to quote them and share their story. Then get their testimonial. That's it.

It is smart to ask them if you can share their name with others as well, just to be on the safe side. At least determine their preferences here; never assume anything.

If you do nothing else, just collect testimonials from customers who are in heat and have just expressed how appreciative they are of you and your services.

Another good time is when you "save the day". Did you do something for a customer that was out of the ordinary? Maybe you made an emergency house call at 8:30 at night to fix a small leak, free of charge. Or perhaps they wanted something that was supposedly discontinued, but you went the extra mile and tracked down what they were looking for (even if it were with one of your competitors).

Anytime you save the day, just ask them for a testimonial. In fact, I intentionally look for opportunities to save the day, because it serves in my self interest. If I go the extra mile, then I know they'll give me one heck of a testimonial! Once again, great word of mouth marketing.

Once you get good at the first two, consider putting out a customer survey once in a while. Postcard surveys are inexpensive and quick. If you run a restaurant, this can be done easily at the table or counter. Other businesses may need to send them by mail. Offer an incentive if they return the survey promptly.

To glean testimonials out of this, have the customer answer a few key questions. Then, retype those answers in a letter format, and ask them to sign off on it as a testimonial that you can share with others, with their permission, of course.

There are more aggressive ways to get testimonials, and I would encourage you to be aggressive about getting them, especially after you've gotten the knack for getting the low hanging fruit. Once you get used to asking your "hot" customers and those for whom you've saved the day, experiment with actively seeking out testimonials to further prove your case.

HOW TO USE TESTIMONIALS FOR MAXIMUM EFFECT

I am going to share some examples that you can literally knock off and use in your own business. You can also use them for brainstorming purposes on your own ideas

Let's return to the phone book advertising example. Instead of the typical puffery, your ad might include something that says in effect:

"Look, any business can say that they care about the customer and that they are dependable and have high quality service. Instead of us tooting our own horn, maybe you'd rather hear it from some of our customers themselves. Just call our 'satisfied customer hot line' to hear a pre-recorded message of what our customers think about our services."

You know how much a voice mail account costs? About $4 per month. For $4 a month, you can have a recording of your best customers. How do you get these recordings?

Perhaps you have your sales reps call your customers a few days after the sale. Explain to the customer that for quality issues, would it be okay if you recorded the call? This can be done inexpensively with a digital phone recorder that costs less than $50, or through an online service for about $10 a month.

Then, ask them what their thoughts were on the service or for the product. At the end, ask them if it would be okay if you shared their thoughts with other customers who might be interested in the products or services. You might offer the customer another incentive for this.

That's just one way to get your testimonials recorded. There are others.

Now you have a tool. You have people talking about how good you are. You can put this prerecorded message into all of your marketing communications! Your believability goes through the roof.

Something else you might want to consider is to compile a "testimonial booklet".

Do you know any other salesperson that has a testimonial booklet? Wouldn't that distinguish you from every other competitor out there? I guarantee it does—and in a good way!

Let's say you really went the extra mile and totally knock it out of the park for a customer. They were so happy they called you up and thanked you personally, and said they were so impressed with you because you went above and beyond the call of duty.

This is a golden opportunity to ask them if it would be okay to feature them as case study in your next advertisement. Then you could write an advertisement that really looks like an article, where you simply tell the story of what you did for this customer. This type of advertisement is about a million times more effective than "BUY MY PRODUCT!" advertisements you currently see everywhere you look.

At the very least, you should include some testimonials in your advertising, just to enhance your claims.

One person I knew went as far as video recording his customers' testimonials. Then, when someone didn't purchase the first time they came into his store, five days later they'd get the video in the mail that contained all these wonderful customer testimonials.

Needless to say, there were customers that came back and ended up purchasing who otherwise would probably not have. While that brave technique is not for everyone, it was certainly effective for my colleague.

THE ANATOMY OF A GOOD TESTIMONIAL

Now, some people have tried testimonials and have told me that they don't work. That reminds me of my mom telling me five years ago that her DVD player didn't work. I asked, "Did you plug it in?"

Oops...

Testimonials are like anything else—if you do them poorly they probably will not work. In order to do them right, you must know what a good testimonial looks like.

Here is a not-so-hot testimonial:

"You did a good job!"

Here's a great testimonial:

> "You responded to our call and made it to our house in 7 minutes. The last guys took 2 hours. Not only that, you helped us save 13% off the cost. Thanks a bunch!" Dennis K., Family Counselor, Pineville, KY.

The difference is obvious. Bad testimonials are bland and really don't say anything of specific value. Good testimonials are specific, and give hard facts. I love it when someone says to me: "I read your book on Thursday, and by Saturday morning I did one thing I learned on page 35 that resulted in me making $15,867.13 in profit by the following Tuesday. You're a genius!"

That is a far better testimonial than "your suggestions helped my business."

Not only are specifics needed, but it's good to have a name, location and occupation. Otherwise people will think that maybe you're just making up the testimonials yourself, even though that is illegal (which is why audio and video testimonials are the best).

There are other things that can influence your testimonials. What's better—five testimonials featured in your ads from blue collar males aged 43 and over, or a mix of ages, races and both males and females?

Well, it depends. If your product targets blue collar males that are 43 years old, then it's a good idea. If it targets a wide variety of audiences, then you want testimonials from a wide variety of people.

Lastly, as humans we are hardwired by nature to trust authority. That's why testimonials from scientists, doctors, nurses, fire fighters, and other esteemed positions tend to have more social pull than regular testimonials. Just think how credible a testimonial must be in relation to the product or services you are selling.

So set a plan in action. Come up with the different ways you're going to capture and use testimonials, and make sure everybody in your business starts to become a testimonial collector. It really is one of the easiest ways to increase your sales closing percentage.

If You Must Place Printed Ads...

Have you noticed that 95% of phone book ads look the same? There's a problem with going with the norm—you risk getting normal results, if any.

With your business and livelihood on the line, I hope you are not content with ordinary results, especially when extraordinary results are so easy to obtain, even with phone book or newspaper advertising. You only need to do a few simple things differently.

The first thing you have to understand is what people are looking for when they open up the newspaper or phone book. Some people are looking for specific contact information. If they already have a specific service provider in mind, it's hard to woo those people over (not saying it can't be done).

But the good news is when most people open up the Yellow Pages, for instance, they are looking for information to help them find the best business to contact that will give them the solution they desire.

And here's what consumers want:

- They want a good deal

- They want to do business with someone who is able to understand their needs and lead them to the best solution

- They want to deal with as little headaches, delays and customer service problems as possible.

Now, flip open to the ads section in your phone book and see if any of the ads address the above criteria. You will most likely find that hardly any of them do adequately.

Good. That will make it much easier for you.

I am going to show you how to create a simple print ad that will make people believe that if they contact you or go into your store that they are going to get the best solution for their dollars. Let them know it will be easy and convenient to deal with you and that you're the best choice for all of their options.

If you can pull that off, then you are going to get the lion's share of customers searching in the back of the phonebook or in newspapers for help in your industry.

THE MOST IMPORTANT PART OF YOUR AD

The world's best ad is no better than the world's worst ad if no one sees it. So the first job a printed ad must do is grab the attention of the people who are best matched to take advantage of the services and products that you offer.

The easiest way to do that is with a good attention-getting **headline**.

To understand what a good headline looks like, let's first look at some bad headlines. I went through my own local Yellow Pages, and found these headlines:

"The Blind Factory"

"Cyclists Serving Cyclists"

"Wet Basement or Crawl Space"

"Quality Construction"

"Professional Muffler, Inc"

"Old Fashioned Values, Including Our Own People Doing the Work"

These are all terrible headlines.

Almost all of them talk about the service provider, and not the person who is seeking specific services. Talk about self-centered! Advertisements are supposed to be all about the *customer* and *their* needs, remember?

None of them promise any benefit to the customer; none of them get the person reading excited about their services, and most are nothing more than the name of the company. The customer must be able to say, "There! That's the one for me!" when they see the right ad.

Finally, respect your headline. It is the most important part of your ad so you need to do better than the rest. Ideally, you want a headline that promises a benefit to the reader, and is written to grab the attention of a certain large segment of the population who is best matched for the goods and services you provide.

Let's look at the first one: "The Blind Factory"

How could this one be improved? Here is a good headline that I have found to get great results: "The Five Mistakes Most People Make When They Purchase Blinds for Their Home".

Or: "Warning: Don't Buy Any Blinds Until You Read This". Or Even "How to Get the Best Blinds For You Home in 48 Hours Or Less, Guaranteed!"

Notice the difference with these headlines? First, it's important to note that they focus on the consumer and their particular needs. Second, they promise a huge benefit. Third, they call out a certain segment of the general population. In this case they are addressing people who are looking to purchase blinds, who want to get a good deal, want ease of service, or want to make sure they don't commit a mistake when buying blinds.

Once you have a good headline, the ad practically writes itself. For example, let's return to the headline: "The Five Mistakes People Make When They Purchase Blinds for Their Home". You would then identify 5 mistakes that you find people tend to make if they don't have an expert to help them select their product. And then, after you introduce each mistake, explain how that mistake can be avoided if they come into your store.

Remember, people who turn to the ad sections are generally looking for information to help them make the right decision on finding the best service provider. Typically the person who provides the most information wins—and it helps if that information is beneficial to the reader and strictly focused on their immediate needs.

If you do a quick review of a typical printed ad, you will note that it has 50 words or less, and is usually filled with puffery. For example, I always see "The customer comes first." I say talk to the hand, or prove it!

Which leads us to the second biggest point about writing effective printed ads: Making powerful, unique claims to demonstrate that you provide the services better than any other solution that is available.

How can you make a unique claim that demonstrates that the customer *truly* comes first? Here is a technique that has been used to great effect. The first thing on the list is to contact some of your past satisfied customers. Then, you ask them to write a quick one paragraph testimonial about what they liked most about dealing with your company. It's easy to do this with the strategies we have discussed.

Then, put those testimonials on a website. Now, in your ad you can say, "You can even read what 117 satisfied customers had to say about our great products at www.whatever-your-site.com" and invite traffic to your website in this manner.

Now, people looking at the ad may not visit your website, but it will have the effect of demonstrating to them that not only does the customer truly come first, but you have 117 of your own customers who claim that you *do* put them first. Yours will be the only ad in your category that can claim that, so in a potential customer's mind you would be the preferred source if customer service is their main priority.

Your ad should contain at least one dramatic example of proof to validate your claims. It's best if you have specific numbers or facts to verify it, testimonials to show and other powerful ways to demonstrate that you offer great service and goods, and that you follow through on your end of the bargain.

For example, you can do much better than merely stating something like "In business since 1972!" My first reaction when I see this statement is "So what does that mean for me and my immediate needs?"

The fact is I know several bad companies that have somehow managed to stay shakily in business for decades. Instead, you can say "We've successfully helped over 10,678 clients in Marion find just the right blinds for their home."

So first come up with a powerful headline. Then expand on that headline in your ad. Also remember to throw in at least one dramatic example of proof to validate your claims.

One more thing to note, and avoid. Surprisingly, I often see an ad placed for a business or organizationbut I cannot find an address or phone number on the ad space.

The ad is essentially your billboard. Make sure the information is there—and clear as day.

Now you have one final thing to secure:

HAVE AN OFFER AND A "CALL TO ACTION"

Every single ad, regardless of the media in which it appears, must have an offer and a call-to-action to accept that offer. A call to action means that you tell the customer exactly what they need to do immediately after reading the ad in order to take advantage of it.

Let me start with the best call to action, although it is also the most complicated one to set up.

You ideally want to establish a continuing relationship with people who are interested in doing business with you, so if they are hesitant initially further communication can get them in the door.

The best way to do that is to offer something free to the user if they contact you. Here's a simple way of doing that. Let's go back to the window blinds example.

The first thing you should do is to write a focused report on "How to Pick The Most Beautiful Blinds for Your Home on a Shoestring Budget" (or something to that effect). Your marketing consultant can help you with any copywriting services you need. Using the valuable information contained in the report, offer the customer the best tips for getting the most value from their purchase.

Save the report in PDF format so that it can be used in an autoresponder that you can send to your customers via email later. This allows you to have people sign up for an email list and you can send them email offers in the future.

When people sign up for your list, they will automatically receive your free digital report on "How to Pick The Most Beautiful Blinds for Your Home on a Shoestring Budget." Not only that, you can use an email auto responder to send a few follow up messages automatically at certain intervals to anyone who signs up.

In your ads you say, "If you would like to receive our free report on "How to Pick The Most Beautiful Blinds for Your Home on a Shoestring Budget" visit our website at www.what-ever-your-site.com." This drives them to a page that explains that in order to get the report they just have to enter in their name and email into the form.

Of course, in the report you will list your contact information so the potential customer can easily contact you and become your regular customer.

This is by far the best strategy but also the most complex. A simple strategy is to make a "This Ad Only" offer. In this case you say, "If you call today and schedule an appointment, mention this particular ad and we'll give you a special discounted 20% off any one item."

In any case, you are *enticing* them to respond to your ad.

If you do all of the things in this report, then you are going to have an ad that is dramatically different than everyone else's which will allow you to get dramatically better results!

94

Proven Internet Strategies to Explode Your Local Sales

1 VIDEO MARKETING

Would you believe that there are over 26 *billion* videos viewed per month in the United States alone? What's more, YouTube is the #4 search engine on the internet, which means that right this minute somebody could be searching for your services online in the form of a video.

Imagine if you had the advertising budget to run infomercials 24 hours a day, 7 days a week—you would dominate your market! That's the power of video marketing. This is possible on a shoestring (even in a rough economy) and you can create more trust and respect with your customers than ever before.

A marketing video can be in the form of a simple Power Point presentation or full blown videography. Since more and more people are turning to the Internet to quickly search for information, the use of video is an effective means of capturing the customer's attention by delivering the information quickly and easily.

By using video in your marketing and advertising campaigns, you are able to demonstrate the use of a particular product in a virtual setting. Just remember that the search engines are attracted to videos, so prepare for more traffic to your site. Keep your videos short, sweet, and to the point as to avoid boredom and the eventual fleeing of the viewer. Two minutes run-time is a good rule of thumb for an online video.

A marketing professional can assist you with getting your site ranked with the Search Engine Optimization (SEO) techniques. Remember that the purpose of a video is to promote your business, to capture views of potential customers and, hopefully, the conversion into sales.

#2 INTERNET LEAD-CAPTURE AND FOLLOW-UP CAMPAIGNS

Did you know that even a great webpage will only convert, at best, 5% of its visitors to make a purchase? It's absolutely true, and this means that 19 out of 20 visitors to your website are destined to surf away into the ether world, and could stumble across your competitor's website instead.

However the average page that offers consumers free information in exchange for their contact info gets 35-40% conversion. That is significantly more substantial, which validates the importance of your offer of a free written report. They visit your site; you offer a free report or eBook; they must enter their name and email address (more if you so require) in order to receive it, and voila! You have the beginnings of your email list of customers.

Imagine being able to instantly increase your return on leads seven-fold, and do it with push button automation. This is possible, and a good marketing professional can help you do just that.

This is a great way to capture leads as discussed previously. Engage your marketing consultant or a copywriter for assistance if writing isn't your thing. After all, your time and talents are best used running a successful business.

3 LOCAL INTERNET SEARCH PRESENCE & VISIBILITY

Did you know that 30% of all searches online include a city or local term (for example: "Pineville Plumbing Contractors")? Local consumers will search for local services.

This means that every search for every term will have the local companies that have figured out how to get listed in all of the local directories. The SEO aspect of the Internet can be quite daunting. You must utilize the most powerful and targeted keywords that pertain to your business, services or products.

It goes without saying that your customers cannot hire you if they cannot find you. Once again, your marketer can help make sure that your local business is found on Google, Bing, Yahoo and other search engines when a potential customer types in appropriate keywords that fit your business. This affects how you rank so that your neighbors can easily find you online.

If you are well versed in all things Internet, you may be able to tackle this one yourself. My best advice, my friend, is to concentrate on running your business successfully and let your marketing professional handle the complicated strategies of internet advertising. It is easy to lose valuable time and money if you are not well versed in this media.

4 SOCIAL MEDIA MARKETING

A little blue birdie recently told me that if you aren't tweet, tweeting you may be cheat, cheating yourself out of a huge opportunity in your marketing strategies for your business. The popularity of Facebook, Twitter and blogs (web logs) has forced the issue and it's time to take notice. A savvy business marketer will take full advantage of these media types.

Social media is any media that uses a web-based technology to facilitate social interaction. It appears that we are quickly evolving from a digital world where information was the marketable commodity, to a communications market where new methods of communicating, networking and socializing are being introduced on a rapid fire basis. Blogs, wikis, RSS newsfeeds, podcasts, video socialization built around applications like Facebook, Twitter and YouTube are recently formulated methods of communication that seemingly overnight have developed with literally hundreds of millions of active participants.

With various types of social media literally at your fingertips, you have access to a low cost, highly effective means of spreading your message to a large audience, for fun or for business.

With over 500,000,000 active members, Facebook is a giant that will not be ignored—and it isn't going away any time soon. Social networks have changed the way people research and make their buying decisions. The advertising opportunities are truly astronomical! You have the capability to create laser targeted ads tweaked down to the age, birthdate, likes and dislikes of your customers. Unlimited! And that's only the tip of the iceberg.

This being said, you still need to identify methods that are most appropriate for your target audience and business entity.

When a solid internet presence is leveraged properly in your favor you will have the opportunity to build more trust, respect, and credibility with your customers than ever before.

Imagine being able to have feedback on how to improve your business, and sell more on a daily basis. Imagine being able to turn every customer into a potential raving "Fan" that will "Like" you and will advertise for you. As mentioned earlier, putting it all together can be a bit daunting. But a good marketing professional can make that happen. (Thanks to the internet you can secure my services exclusively in your local market no matter where you are! —or wherever I may roam!).

5   BLOG MARKETING

It is said that 77% of all internet users follow one or more blogs (web log). If you are not capitalizing on this growing community, you are missing out on more advertising opportunities, reaching more of the masses.

A blog is often a blend between what is occurring on the web, in the marketplace, or in one's life. Bloggers, sometimes also called Infopreneurs these days, are passionate about sharing what they love, and if you have one as a client and can turn them into a raving Fan, they can propel your business to new heights.

A blog is very easy to set up and maintain. It's a great way to open the conversation with potential customers and gain valuable insights to buying habits.

You can join a blog already in progress or start your own. Wordpress.com, Blogger.com and Blog.com are among the most used blogs though there are many others that are free and fairly user friendly.

Blogs are useful for the sake of business in that you can obtain customer leads through them as well as place affiliate ads and links on your page which means you earn a commission if a product is sold from your site. But blogs are great for personal use, too. You can practice your writing; encourage thought provoking conversation, whatever...you name it.

It's your blog...do what you want to do! And you will be surprised at how many other people visit your little corner of the World Wide Web.

Conclusion

The goal of laser-targeted advertising is obviously to increase your bottom line profits year after year. I hope you afford yourself every opportunity to think 'outside of the box' and get in step with today's competitive, sometimes complicated, local marketing environment. You *can* easily out-do your competitors! Use every advantage I have given you in this book to create your own work of *art—* your creative marketing masterpiece.

To accent your marketing endeavors, look for the right marketing professional best suited to assist you and your unique business needs. They must listen to you intently, exude creativity and be well-versed in today's complicated marketing strategies. I'm not saying it can't be done, but it can be extremely daunting for a business owner or manager to handle advertising alone, when your time and talents are better used for the running of your business.

The internet has indeed made the globe shrink in the virtual sense. You have immediate access to, and can communicate with, individuals in every time zone around the planet at any given moment in time.

Take advantage of mobile marketing techniques, first and foremost. Your customers are virtually at your fingertips! Send out a text blast when business is slow, or there was an appointment cancellation that can be refilled by another client waiting anxiously to take their place.

The restaurant crowds can catch the busy family rush and students during the mid-week, or the football fanatics on Sunday afternoons by offering specials to get them in the door. To add to the fun and frolic on game day (or during a political election), you can arrange to sponsor cell phone surveys or voting polls among your clientele. The possibilities are endless.

In today's economy and tough competitive marketplace, your customers will acknowledge your added attention to detail for them. They appreciate and count on special offers and coupons from their favorite businesses. They *want* to give you their commerce.

Hone your art of local advertising. By making it worth their while, customers enjoy the discount they receive and you get the additional business you need.

No matter how you chalk it up, that's a win-win!

About the Author

Author, speaker and experienced marketing consultant, Connie Gorrell is an expert at helping businesses gain a dominant position in their local marketplace. As CEO of Concierge Custom and Mobile Marketing, Connie knows the importance of strategic planning based on individual needs and market analysis.

As a former healthcare professional and educator, Connie enjoys helping other entrepreneurs and small businesses gain a competitive advantage in their local marketplace. She specializes in mobile and social marketing strategies for her coveted clients. As an expert copywriter, Connie creates unique and customized ads both for print or online services.

Connie's philosophy is "under-promise and over-deliver" when it comes to customer satisfaction and teaches various methods in workshops. She stresses the importance that businesses are easily located on the Internet, that they take necessary steps to never run out of leads, and transforms potential clients into lifetime customers and raving "Fans" that "Like" them immensely!

Connie enjoys hearing from her readers. If you have concerns about how to improve your business' bottom line or questions regarding any of the strategies listed in this book, please refer to the *Contact Us* section at www.conciergemobilemarketing.com, or email her at congorrell@gmail.com.

Made in the USA
Charleston, SC
26 March 2012